It was sunny on Sunday.

It was cloudy on Monday.

It was rainy on Tuesday.

It was windy on Wednesday.

It was foggy on Thursday.

It was snowy on Friday and Saturday.

Weather Report

Sunday

sunny

Monday

cloudy

Tuesday

rainy

Wednesday

windy

Thursday

foggy

Friday
Saturday

snowy

✿ Ideas for guided reading ✿

Learning objectives: know that print carries meaning and is read from left to right; blend letters to read words and recognise common digraphs; sustain attentive listening, responding to what they have heard

Curriculum links: Knowledge and Understanding of the World: Find out about and identify some features of events they observe; Creative Development: Respond in a variety of ways to what they see, hear, smell, touch and feel

High frequency words: it, was, on, and

Interest words: Monday, Tuesday, Wednesday, Thursday, Friday, Saturday, Sunday, sunny, cloudy, rainy, windy, foggy, snowy

Resources: whiteboards, pens, musical instruments

Word count: 32

Getting started

- Look at the weather today and discuss words to describe it.
- Make a note of weather words in a cloud shape drawn on the whiteboard.
- Skim through the book looking at the photographs, and decide what kind of weather is pictured in each one.
- Return to the title page and read the title together, pointing to the words.
- Read the book together, pointing to each word in turn and encouraging the children to name the day of the week.

Reading and responding

- Ask the children to read independently, and to try reading the words they are unsure of.
- Direct early finishers to read the book to each other.
- Turn to p7. What is the girl doing? What do they like to do when it's rainy?